Tom Gourdie
4 . 7 . 95 .

# The Sonnets of Shakespeare

\*

Transcribed in the Sweet Roman Hand

\*

Tom Gourdie

\*

CASSELL · LONDON

Cassell Publishers Limited
Artillery House, Artillery Row
London SW1P 1RT

First published 1988

**British Library Cataloguing in Publication Data**
Shakespeare, William
    [Sonnets].   The sonnets of Shakespeare:
    transcribed in the sweet Roman hand.
    I. [Sonnets]   II. Title   II. Gourdie, Tom.
    821′.3     PR2848

ISBN 0 304 32171 0

Printed and bound in Great Britain by The Bath Press

To my wife,
Lilias,
and in memory of
our daughter,
Lilias Isabel,
( 1943 – 79 )

# The Sonnets

FROM·FAIREST·CREATURES we desire increase
That thereby beauty's rose might never die
But as the riper should by time decease
His tender heir might bear his memory:
But thou, contracted to thine own bright eyes,
Feed'st thy light's flame with self-substantial fuel,
Making a famine where abundance lies,
Thyself thy foe, to thy sweet self too cruel:
Thou that are now the world's fresh ornament,
And only herald to the gaudy spring,
Within thine own bud buriest thy content,
And tender churl mak'st waste in niggarding:
    Pity the world, or else this glutton be,
    To eat the world's due, by the grave and thee.

Sonnet No 1

WHEN · FORTY · WINTERS shall besiege thy brow,
And dig deep trenches in thy beauty's field,
Thy youth's proud livery, so gazed on now,
Will be'a tattered weed of small worth held.
Then being asked where'all thy beauty lies,
Where'all the'treasure of thy lusty days,
To say within thine'own deep sunken eyes
Were'an all-eating shame'and thriftless praise.
How much more'praise'deserved thy beauty's use'
If thou couldst answer 'This fair child of mine'
Shall sum my count and make'my old excuse,'
Proving his beauty by succession thine.'
  This were'to be'new made'when thou art old,
  And see thy blood warm when thou feel'st it cold.

Sonnet No 2

LOOK·IN·THY·GLASS and tell the face thou viewest

Now is the time that face should form another

Whose fresh repair if now thou not renewest

Thou dost beguile the world, unbless some mother.

For where is she so fair whose uneared womb

Disdains the tillage of thy husbandry?

Or who is he so fond will be the tomb

Of his self-love to stop posterity?

Thou art thy mother's glass, and she in thee

Calls back the lovely April of her prime;

So thou through windows of thine age shalt see,

Despite of wrinkles, this thy golden time.

But if thou live remembered not to be,

Die single, and thine image dies with thee.

Sonnet No 3

UNTHRIFTY·LOVELINESS, why dost thou spend
Upon thyself thy beauty's legacy?
Nature's bequest gives nothing, but doth lend,
And being frank she lends to those are free.
Then, beauteous niggard, why dost thou abuse
The bounteous largess given thee to give?
Profitless usurer, why dost thou use
So great a sum of sums yet canst not live?
For having traffic with thyself alone
Thou of thyself thy sweet self dost deceive;
Then how when Nature calls thee to be gone,
What acceptable audit canst thou leave?
    Thy unused beauty must be tombed with thee,
    Which, used, lives th'executor to be.

Sonnet No 4

THOSE·HOURS that with gentle work did frame
The lovely gaze where every eye doth dwell
Will play the tyrants to the very same
And that unfair which fairly doth excel;
For never-resting Time leads summer on
To hideous winter and confounds him there,
Sap checked with frost and lusty leaves quite gone,
Beauty o'ersnowed and bareness everywhere:
Then, were not summer's distillation left
A liquid prisoner pent in walls of glass,
Beauty's effect with beauty were bereft,
Nor it nor no remembrance what it was.
But flowers distilled, though they with winter meet,
Leese but their show, their substance still lives sweet.

Sonnet No 5

THEN·LET·NOT·WINTER'S ragged hand deface
In thee thy summer ere thou be distilled.
Make sweet some vial: treasure thou some place
With beauty's treasure ere it be self-killed.
That use is not forbidden usury
Which happies those that pay the willing loan ~
That's for thyself to breed another thee,
Or ten times happier be it ten for one.
Ten times thyself were happier than thou art,
If ten of thine ten times refigured thee;
Then what could death do if thou shouldst depart,
Leaving thee living in posterity?
    Be not self-willed, for thou art much too fair
    To be death's conquest and make worms thine heir.

Sonnet No 6

**L**O IN·THE·ORIENT when the gracious light
, Lifts up his burning head, each under eye
 Doth homage to his new-appearing sight,
Serving with looks his sacred majesty;
And having climbed the steep-up heavenly hill,
Resembling strong youth in his midde age,
Yet mortal looks adore his beauty still,
Attending on his golden pilgrimage;
But when from highmost pitch, with weary car,
Like feeble age he reeleth from the day,
The eyes, fore duteous, now converted are
From his low tract and look another way:
 So thou, thyself outgoing in thy noon,
 Unlooked on diest unless thou get a son.

Sonnet No 7

MUSIC·TO·HEAR, why hear'st thou music sadly?
Sweets with sweets war not, joy delights in joy;
Why lov'st thou that which thou receiv'st not gladly,
Or else receiv'st with pleasure thine annoy?
If the true concord of well-tunèd sounds,
By unions married, do offend thine ear,
They do but sweetly chide thee, who confounds
In singleness the parts that thou shouldst bear.
Mark how one string, sweet husband to another,
Strikes each in each by mutual ordering;
Resembling sire, and child, and happy mother,
Who, all in one, one pleasing note do sing;
Whose speechless song, being many, seeming one,
Sings this to thee: 'Thou single wilt prove none.'

Sonnet No 8

IS·IT·FOR·FEAR to wet a widow's eye
  That thou consum'st thyself in single life'?
  Ah, if thou issueless shalt hap to die'
The' world will wail thee' like' a makeless wife';
The' world will be' thy widow and still weep
That thou no form of thee' hast left behind,
When every private' widow well may keep
By children's eyes her husband's shape' in mind.
Look what an unthrift in the' world doth spend,
Shifts but his place', for still the' world enjoys it;
But beauty's waste' hath in the' world an end,
And kept unused, the' user so destroys it.
    No love' toward others in that bosom sits
    That on himself such murd'rous shame' commits.

FOR·SHAME, deny that thou bear'st love to any,
Who for thyself art so unprovident!
Grant if thou wilt, thou art beloved of many,
But that thou none lov'st is most evident;
For thou art so possessed with murd'rous hate,
That 'gainst thyself thou stick'st not to conspire,
Seeking that beauteous roof to ruinate,
Which to repair should be thy chief desire.
O, change thy thought, that I may change my mind!
Shall hate be fairer lodged than gentle love?
Be as thy presence is, gracious and kind,
Or to thyself at least kind-hearted prove:
Make thee another self for love of me,
That beauty still may live in thine or thee.

Sonnet No 10

AS FAST·AS·THOU·SHALT wane, so fast thou grow'st
In one of thine from that which thou departest;
And that fresh blood which youngly thou bestow'st
Thou mayst call thine, when thou from youth convertest.
Herein lives wisdom, beauty, and increase;
Without this, folly, age, and cold decay.
If all were minded so, the times should cease,
And three score year would make the world away.
Let those whom Nature hath not made for store—
Harsh, featureless, and rude—barrenly perish.
Look whom she best endowed she gave the more;
Which bounteous gift thou shouldst in bounty cherish.
She carved thee for her seal, and meant thereby
Thou shouldst print more, nor let that copy die.

Sonnet No 11

WHEN·I·DO·COUNT the clock that tells the time,
And see the brave day sunk in hideous night;
When I behold the violet past prime,
And sable curls all silvered o'er with white;
When lofty trees I see barren of leaves,
Which erst from heat did canopy the herd,
And summer's green, all girded up in sheaves,
Borne on the bier with white and bristly beard;
Then of thy beauty do I question make,
That thou among the wastes of time must go,
Since sweets and beauties do themselves forsake,
And die as fast as they see others grow;
    And nothing 'gainst Time's scythe can make defence
    Save breed to brave him when he takes thee hence.

Sonnet No 12

**O** THAT·YOU·WERE·YOURSELF; but, love, you are
No longer yours than you yourself here live.
Against this coming end you should prepare,
And your sweet semblance to some other give.
So should that beauty which you hold in lease
Find no determination; then you were
Yourself again after yourself's decease,
When your sweet issue your sweet form should bear.
Who lets so fair a house fall to decay,
Which husbandry in honour might uphold
Against the stormy gusts of winter's day
And barren rage of death's eternal cold?
O, none but unthrifts! Dear my love, you know
You had a father; let your son say so.

Sonnet No 13

NOT·FROM·THE·STARS do I my judgement pluck,
  And yet methinks I have astronomy;
    But not to tell of good or evil luck,
  Of plagues, of dearths, or seasons' quality;
  Nor can I fortune' to brief minutes tell,
  Pointing to each his thunder, rain and wind,
  Or say with princes if it shall go well
  By oft predict that I in heaven find.
  But from thine' eyes my knowledge' I derive',
  And, constant stars, in them I read such art
  As truth and beauty shall together thrive'
  If from thyself to store' thou wouldst convert;
    Or else' of thee' this I prognosticate,'
    Thy end is truth's and beauty's doom and date.

Sonnet No 14

WHEN·I·CONSIDER every thing that grows
Holds in perfection but a little moment,
That this huge stage presenteth naught but shows
Whereon the stars in secret influence comment;
When I perceive that men as plants increase,
Cheerèd and checked even by the selfsame sky,
Vaunt in their youthful sap, at height decrease,
And wear their brave state out of memory;
Then the conceit of this inconstant stay
Sets you most rich in youth before my sight,
Where wasteful Time debateth with Decay,
To change your day of youth to sullied night;
    And all in war with Time for love of you,
    As he takes from you I engraft you new.

Sonnet No 15

BUT·WHEREFORE do not you a mightier way
Make war upon this bloody tyrant Time,
And fortify yourself in your decay
With means more blessèd than my barren rhyme?
Now stand you on the top of happy hours,
And many maiden gardens, yet unset,
With virtuous wish would bear your living flowers,
Much liker than your painted counterfeit.
So should the lines of life that life repair
Which this time's pencil or my pupil pen
Neither in inward worth nor outward fair
Can make you live yourself in eyes of men.
   To give away yourself keep yourself still,
   And you must live drawn by your own sweet skill.

Sonnet No 16

**W**HO·WILL·BELIEVE my verse in time to come
If it were filled with your most high deserts?
Though yet, heaven knows, it is but as a tomb
Which hides your life and shows not half your parts.
If I could write the beauty of your eyes,
And in fresh numbers number all your graces,
The age to come would say 'This poet lies;
Such heavenly touches ne'er touched earthly faces.'
So should my papers, yellowed with their age,
Be scorned, like old men of less truth than tongue,
And your true rights be termed a poet's rage
And stretchèd metre of an antique song.
   But were some child of yours alive that time,
   You should live twice, in it and in my rhyme.

Sonnet No 17

SHALL·I·COMPARE·THEE to a summer's day?
Thou art more lovely and more temperate.
Rough winds do shake the darling buds of May,
And summer's lease hath all too short a date.
Sometime too hot the eye of heaven shines,
And often is his gold complexion dimmed;
And every fair from fair sometime declines,
By chance or nature's changing course untrimmed.
But that eternal summer shall not fade,
Nor lose possession of that fair thou ow'st,
Nor shall Death brag thou wand'rest in his shade,
When in eternal lines to time thou grow'st.
So long as men can breathe or eyes can see,
So long lives this, and this gives life to thee.

Sonnet No 18

DEVOURING·TIME, blunt thou the lion's paws,
And make the earth devour her own sweet brood;
    Pluck the keen teeth from the fierce tiger's jaws,
And burn the long-lived phoenix in her blood;
Make glad and sorry seasons as thou fleet'st,
And do whate'er thou wilt, swift-footed Time,
To the wide world and all her fading sweets.
But I forbid thee one most heinous crime:
O, carve not with thy hours my love's fair brow,
Nor draw no lines there with thine antique pen;
Him in thy course untainted do allow
For beauty's pattern to succeeding men.
    Yet do thy worst, old Time; despite thy wrong,
    My love shall in my verse ever live young.

Sonnet No 19

A · WOMAN'S · FACE with Nature's own hand painted,
Hast thou, the master-mistress of my passion ;
A woman's gentle heart, but not acquainted
With shifting change, as is false women's fashion;
An eye more bright than theirs, less false in rolling,
Gilding the object whereupon it gazeth;
A man in hue all hues in his controlling,
Which steals men's eyes and women's souls amazeth.
And for a woman wert thou first created,
Till Nature as she wrought thee fell a-doting,
And by addition me of thee defeated,
By adding one thing to my purpose nothing.
But since she pricked thee out for women's pleasure,
Mine be thy love, and thy love's use their treasure.

Sonnet No 20

So·IS·IT·NOT·WITH·ME as with that Muse,
Stirred by a painted beauty to his verse,
Who heaven itself for ornament doth use,
And every fair with his fair doth rehearse,
Making a couplement of proud compare
With sun and moon, with earth and sea's rich gems,
With April's first-born flowers, and all things rare
That heaven's air in this huge rondure hems.
O, let me, true in love, but truly write,
And then, believe me, my love is as fair
As any mother's child, though not so bright
As those gold candles fixed in heaven's air.
Let them say more that like of hearsay well;
I will not praise that purpose not to sell.

Sonnet No 21

Y· GLASS·SHALL ·NOT·PERSUADE me I am old

So long as youth and thou are of one date';

But when in thee' Time's furrows I behold,

Then look I death my days should expiate'.

For all that beauty that doth cover thee'

Is but the'seemly raiment of my heart,

Which in thy breast doth live', as thine' in me'.

How can I then be elder than thou art ?

O, therefore', love', be' of thyself so wary

As I, not for myself, but for thee' will,

Bearing thy heart, which I will keep so chary

As tender nurse' her babe' from faring ill.

Presume' not on thy heart when mine' is slain ;

Thou gav'st me' thine', not to give' back again.

Sonnet No 22

As AN·UNPERFECT·ACTOR on the stage,
Who with his fear is put besides his part,
Or some fierce thing replete with too much rage,
Whose strength's abundance weakens his own heart;
So I, for fear of trust, forget to say
The perfect ceremony of love's rite,
And in mine own love's strength seem to decay,
O'ercharged with burden of mine own love's might.
O, let my books be then the eloquence
And dumb presagers of my speaking breast,
Who plead for love and look for recompense
More than that tongue that more hath more expressed.
O, learn to read what silent love hath writ;
To hear with eyes belongs to love's fine wit.

Sonnet No 23

MINE·EYE· hath played the painter and hath steeled
Thy beauty's form in table of my heart;
My body is the frame wherein 'tis held,
And perspective it is best painter's art;
For through the painter must you see his skill
To find where your true image pictured lies,
Which in my bosom's shop is hanging still,
That hath his windows glazèd with thine eyes.
Now see what good turns eyes for eyes have done:
Mine eyes have drawn thy shape, and thine for me
Are windows to my breast, wherethrough the sun
Delights to peep, to gaze therein on thee.
    Yet eyes this cunning want to grace their art:
    They draw but what they see, know not the heart.

Sonnet No 24

LET·THOSE who are in favour with their stars
Of public honour and proud titles boast,
Whilst I, whom fortune of such triumph bars,
Unlooked for joy in that I honour most.
Great princes' favourites their fair leaves spread
But as the marigold at the sun's eye,
And in themselves their pride lies buried
For at a frown they in their glory die.
The painful warrior famoused for fight,
After a thousand victories once foiled,
Is from the book of honour razèd quite,
And all the rest forgot for which he toiled.
Then happy I that love and am beloved,
Where I may not remove nor be removed.

Sonnet No 25

LORD·OF·MY·LOVE, to whom in vassalage'
Thy merit hath my duty strongly knit,
To thee' I send this written ambassage',
To witness duty, not to show my wit ~
Duty so great, which wit so poor as mine'
May make' seem bare', in wanting words to show it,
But that I hope' some' good conceit of thine'
In thy soul's thought, all naked, will bestow it;
Till whatsoever star that guides my moving
Points on me' graciously with fair aspect,
And puts apparel on my tattered loving
To show me' worthy of thy sweet respect.
    Then may I dare to boast how I do love thee',
    Till then, not show my head where' thou mayst prove me'.

Sonnet No 26

WEARY·WITH·TOIL, I haste me to my bed,
The dear repose for limbs with travel tired;
But then begins a journey in my head
To work my mind when body's work's expired;
For then my thoughts, from far where I abide,
Intend a zealous pilgrimage to thee,
And keep my drooping eyelids open wide,
Looking on darkness which the blind do see';
Save that my soul's imaginary sight
Presents thy shadow to my sightless view,
Which like a jewel hung in ghastly night
Makes black night beauteous and her old face new.
      Lo, thus by day my limbs, by night my mind,
      For thee, and for myself, no quiet find.

Sonnet No 27

HOW·CAN·I·THEN·RETURN in happy plight
That am debarred the benefit of rest,
When day's oppression is not eased by night,
But day by night and night by day oppressed,
And each, though enemies to either's reign,
Do in consent shake hands to torture me,
The one by toil, the other to complain
How far I toil, still farther off from thee?
I tell the day, to please him, thou art bright
And dost him grace when clouds do blot the heaven;
So flatter I the swart-complexioned night,
When sparkling stars twire not, thou gild'st the even.
    But day doth daily draw my sorrows longer,
    And night doth nightly make grief's length seem stronger.

Sonnet No 28

WHEN, IN·DISGRACE with Fortune and men's eyes,
I all alone beweep my outcast state,
And trouble deaf heaven with my bootless cries,
And look upon myself and curse my fate—
Wishing me like to one more rich in hope,
Featured like him, like him with friends possessed,
Desiring this man's art, and that man's scope,
With what I most enjoy contented least;
Yet, in these thoughts myself almost despising,
Haply I think on thee, and then my state,
Like to the lark at break of day arising
From sullen earth, sings hymns at heaven's gate;
　For thy sweet love remembered such wealth brings
　That then I scorn to change my state with kings.

Sonnet No 29

WHEN·TO·THE·SESSIONS of sweet silent thought
I summon up remembrance of things past,
I sigh the lack of many a thing I sought,
And with old woes new wail my dear time's waste;
Then can I drown an eye, unused to flow,
For precious friends hid in death's dateless night,
And weep afresh love's long since cancelled woe,
And moan th'expense of many a vanished sight;
Then can I grieve at grievances foregone,
And heavily from woe to woe tell o'er
The sad account of fore-bemoanèd moan,
Which I new pay as if not paid before.
  But if the while I think on thee, dear friend,
  All losses are restored and sorrows end.

Sonnet No 30

THY·BOSOM·IS·ENDEARĒD with all hearts,
Which I by lacking have supposed dead;
    And there reigns love and all love's loving parts,
And all those friends which I thought burièd.
How many a holy and obsequious tear
Hath dear religious love stol'n from mine eye,
As interest of the dead, which now appear
But things removed that hidden in thee lie'!
Thou art the grave where buried love doth live,
Hung with the trophies of my lovers gone
Who all their parts of me to thee did give;
That due of many now is thine alone.
    Their images I loved I view in thee,
    And thou, all they, hast all the all of me.

Sonnet No 31

IF· THOU·SURVIVE my well-contented day
When that churl Death my bones with dust shall cover,
And shalt by fortune once more re-survey
These poor rude lines of thy deceasèd lover,
Compare them with the bettering of the time,
And though they be outstripped by every pen,
Reserve them for my love, not for their rhyme,
Exceeded by the height of happier men.
O, then vouchsafe me but this loving thought:
'Had my friend's Muse grown with this growing age,
A dearer birth than this his love had brought
To march in ranks of better equipage':
     But since he died, and poets better prove,
     Theirs for their style I'll read, his for his love."

*Sonnet No 32*

FULL·MANY·A·GLORIOUS morning have I seen
Flatter the mountain tops with sovereign eye,
Kissing with golden face the meadows green,
Gilding pale streams with heavenly alchemy,
Anon permit the basest clouds to ride
With ugly rack on his celestial face
And from the forlorn world his visage hide,
Stealing unseen to west with this disgrace:
Even so my sun one early morn did shine
With all triumphant splendour on my brow;
But out alack, he was but one hour mine —
The region cloud hath masked him from me now.
    Yet him for this my love no whit disdaineth:
    Suns of the world may stain when heaven's sun staineth.

Sonnet No 33

WHY·DIDST·THOU· promise such a beauteous day
And make me travel forth without my cloak,
To let base clouds o'ertake me in my way,
Hiding thy brav'ry in their rotten smoke'?
'Tis not enough that through the cloud thou break
To dry the rain on my storm-beaten face,
For no man well of such a salve can speak
That heals the wound and cures not the disgrace'.
Nor can thy shame give physic to my grief;
Though thou repent, yet I have still the loss.
Th'offender's sorrow lends but weak relief
To him that bears the strong offence's cross.
    Ah, but those tears are pearl which thy love sheeds,
    And they are rich and ransom all ill deeds.

Sonnet No 34

NO·MORE·BE·GRIEVED at that which thou hast done:
   Roses have thorns, and silver fountains mud,
   Clouds and eclipses stain both moon and sun,
And loathsome canker lives in sweetest bud.
All men make faults ~ and even I in this:
Authorising thy trespass with compare,
Myself corrupting, salving thy amiss —
Excusing thy sins more than thy sins are;
For to thy sensual fault I bring in sense,
Thy adverse party is thy advocate,
And 'gainst myself a lawful plea commence:
Such civil war is in my love and hate
     That I an accessory needs must be
     To that sweet thief which sourly robs from me.

Sonnet No 35

LET·ME·CONFESS that we two must be twain,
Although our undivided loves are one.
So shall those blots that do with me remain
Without thy help by me be borne alone.
In our two loves there is but one respect,
Though in our lives a separable spite,
Which, though it alter not love's sole effect,
Yet doth it steal sweet hours from love's delight.
I may not evermore acknowledge thee,
Lest my bewailed guilt should do thee shame;
Nor thou with public kindness honour me,
Unless thou take that honour from thy name.
    But do not so : I love thee in such sort
    As, thou being mine, mine is thy good report.

Sonnet No 36

AS A DECREPIT FATHER takes delight
To see his active child do deeds of youth,
So I, made lame by Fortune's dearest spite,
Take all my comfort of thy worth and truth
For whether beauty, birth, or wealth, or wit,
Or any of these all, or all, or more,
Entitled in thy parts do crownèd sit,
I make my love engrafted to this store:
So then I am not lame, poor, nor despised,
Whilst that this shadow doth such substance give
That I in thy abundance am sufficed,
And by a part of all thy glory live.
    Look what is best, that best I wish in thee:
    This wish I have, then ten times happy me!

Sonnet No 37

HOW·CAN·MY·MUSE want subject to invent
While thou dost breathe, that pour'st into my verse
Thine own sweet argument, too excellent
For every vulgar paper to rehearse?
O, give thyself the thanks, if aught in me
Worthy perusal stand against thy sight;
For who's so dumb that cannot write to thee
When thou thyself dost give invention light?
Be thou the tenth Muse, ten times more in worth
Than those old nine which rhymers invocate;
And he that calls on thee, let him bring forth
Eternal numbers to outlive long date.
    If my slight Muse do please these curious days,
    The pain be mine, but thine shall be the praise.

Sonnet No 38

O HOW·THY·WORTH with manners may I sing,
    When thou art all the better part of me?
    What can mine own praise to mine own self bring?
And what is't but mine own when I praise thee?
Even for this let us divided live,
And our dear love lose name of single one,
That by this separation I may give
That due to thee which thou deserv'st alone.
O absence, what a torment wouldst thou prove,
Were it not thy sour leisure gave sweet leave
To entertain the time with thoughts of love,
Which time and thoughts so sweetly dost deceive,
    And that thou teachest how to make one twain,
    By praising him here who doth hence remain!

Sonnet No 39

TAKE·ALL·MY·LOVES, my love, yea, take them all:
What hast thou then more than thou hadst before?
No love, my love, that thou mayst true love call;
All mine was thine, before thou hadst this more.
Then if for my love thou my love receivest,
I cannot blame thee, for my love thou usest;
But yet be blamed, if thou thyself deceivest
By wilful taste of what thyself refusest.
I do forgive thy robb'ry gentle thief,
Although thou steal thee all my poverty;
And yet love knows it is a greater grief
To bear love's wrong, than hate's known injury.
  Lascivious grace in whom all ill well shows,
  Kill me with spites, yet we must not be foes.

Sonnet No 40

THOSE·PRETTY·WRONGS that liberty commits,
   When I am sometime absent from thy heart,
      Thy beauty and thy years full well befits,
For still temptation follows where thou art.
Gentle thou art, and therefore to be won;
Beauteous thou art, therefore to be assailed;
And when a woman woos, what woman's son
Will sourly leave her till she have prevailed?
Ay me, but yet thou might'st my seat forbear,
And chide thy beauty and thy straying youth,
Who lead thee in their riot even there
Where thou are forced to break a twofold truth:
      Hers, by thy beauty tempting her to thee,
      Thine, by thy beauty being false to me.

THAT·THOU·HAST·HER, it is not all my grief,
And yet it may be'said I loved her dearly;
That she'hath thee'is of'my wailing chief,
A loss in love'that touches me'more'nearly.
Loving offenders, thus I will excuse'ye':
Thou dost love'her because'thou know'st I love'her,
And for my sake'even so doth she'abuse'me',
Suff'ring my friend for my sake'to approve'her.
If I lose'thee', my loss is my love's gain,
And, losing her, my friend hath found that loss;
Both find each other, and I lose'both twain,
And both for my sake'lay on me'this cross.
But here's the'joy: my friend and I are one'.
Sweet flatt'ry! Then she'loves but me'alone'!

Sonnet No 42

WHEN·MOST·I·WINK, then do mine eyes best see,
    For all the day they view things unrespected;
    But when I sleep, in dreams they look on thee,
And, darkly bright, are bright in dark directed.
Then thou, whose shadow shadows doth make bright,
How would thy shadow's form form happy show
To the clear day with thy much clearer light
When to unseeing eyes thy shade shines so!
How would, I say, mine eyes be blessèd made,
By looking on thee in the living day,
When in dead night thy fair imperfect shade
Through heavy sleep on sightless eyes doth stay!
    All days are nights to see till I see thee,
    All nights bright days when dreams do show thee me.

Sonnet No 43

**IF** THE·DULL·SUBSTANCE of my flesh were thought,
Injurious distance should not stop my way;
For then despite of space I would be brought,
From limits far remote, where thou dost stay.
No matter then although my foot did stand
Upon the farthest earth removed from thee;
For nimble thought can jump both sea and land
As soon as think the place where he would be.
But ah, thought kills me that I am not thought,
To leap large lengths of miles when thou art gone,
But that, so much of earth and water wrought,
I must attend time's leisure with my moan;
   Receiving naught by elements so slow
   But heavy tears, badges of either's woe.

Sonnet No 44

THE·OTHER·TWO, slight air and purging fire,
Are both with thee wherever I abide;
The first my thought, the other my desire,
These present-absent with swift motion slide;
For when these quicker elements are gone
In tender embassy of love to thee,
My life, being made of four, with two alone
Sinks down to death, oppressed with melancholy
Until life's composition be recured
By those swift messengers returned from thee,
Who even but now come back again, assured
Of thy fair health, recounting it to me:
    This told, I joy; but then no longer glad
    I send them back again, and straight grow sad.

Sonnet No 45

INE·EYE·AND·HEART are at a mortal war
How to divide the conquest of thy sight;
Mine eye, my heart thy picture's sight would bar
Mine heart, mine eye the freedom of that right:
My heart doth plead that thou in him dost lie
A closet never pierced with crystal eyes,
But the defendant doth that plea deny,
And says in him thy fair appearance lies.
To 'cide this title is impanellèd
A quest of thoughts, all tenants to the heart,
And by their verdict is determinèd
The clear eye's moiety and the dear heart's part.
    As thus: mine eye's due is thine outward part,
    And my heart's right, thine inward love of heart.

Sonnet No 46

BETWIXT·MINE·EYE and heart a league'is took,
And each doth good turns now unto the'other,
When that mine'eye'is famish'd for a look,
Or heart in love'with sighs himself doth smother;
With my love's picture then my eye'doth feast,
And to the'painted banquet bids my heart:
Another time'mine'eye'is my heart's guest,
And in his thoughts of love'doth share a part.
So either by thy picture or my love',
Thyself away, art present still with me',
For thou not farther than my thoughts canst move',
And I am still with them, and they with thee'.
Or if they sleep, thy picture in my sight
Awakes my heart, to heart's and eye's delight.

Sonnet No 47

HOW·CAREFUL·WAS·I· when I took my way,
Each trifle under truest bars to thrust,
That to my use it might unused stay
From hands of falsehood, in sure wards of trust?
But thou, to whom my jewels trifles are,
Most worthy comfort, now my greatest grief,
Thou best of dearest, and mine only care,
Art left the prey of every vulgar thief.
Thee have I not locked up in any chest,
Save where thou art not, though I feel thou art,
Within the gentle closure of my breast,
From whence at pleasure thou mayst come and part;
  And even thence thou wilt be stolen, I fear,
  For truth proves thievish for a prize so dear.

Sonnet No 48

AGAINST·THAT·TIME (*if ever that time come*)
   When I shall see thee frown on my defects,
   Whenas thy love hast cast his utmost sum,
Called to that audit by advised respects:
Against that time when thou shalt strangely pass,
And scarcely greet me with that sun thine eye,
When love converted from the thing it was
Shall reasons find of settled gravity.
Against that time do I ensconce me here
Within the knowledge of mine own desert,
And this my hand, against myself uprear,
To guard the lawful reasons on thy part,
      To leave poor me thou hast the strength of laws,
      Since why to love I can allege no cause.

Sonnet No 49

HOW·HEAVY·DO·I·JOURNEY·ON·THE·WAY
When what I seek (my weary travel's end)
Doth teach that ease and that repose to say
Thus far the miles are measured from thy friend.
The beast that bears me, tired with my woe,
Plods dully on, to bear that weight in me,
As if by some instinct the wretch did know
His rider lov'd not speed being made from thee:
The bloody **spur** cannot provoke him on,
That sometimes anger thrusts into his hide,
Which heavily he answers with a groan,
More sharp to me than spurring to his side,
    For that same groan doth put this in my mind,
    My grief lies onward and my joy behind.

Sonnet No 50

THUS·CAN·MY·LOVE excuse the slow offence
Of my dull bearer, when from thee I speed:
From where thou art, why should I haste me thence?
Till I return of posting is no need.
O what excuse will my poor beast then find,
When swift extremity can seem but slow?
Then should I spur though mounted on the wind;
In wingèd speed no motion shall I know.
Then can no horse with my desire keep pace;
Therefore desire, of perfect'st love being made,
Shall neigh, no dull flesh in his fiery race;
But love, for love, thus shall excuse my jade:
    Since from thee going he went wilful slow,
    Towards thee I'll run, and give him leave to go.

Sonnet No 51

**S** AM·I·AS·THE·RICH·WHOSE·BLESSED·KEY

Can bring him to his sweet up-lockèd treasure,

The which he'will not every hour survey,

For blunting the'fine'point of seldom pleasure.

Therefore are feasts so solemn and so rare,

Since, seldom coming, in the long year set,

Like'stones of worth they thinly placèd are,

Or captain jewels in the'carcanet.

So is the'time'that keeps you as my chest,

Or as the'wardrobe'which the'robe'doth hide,

To make'some'special instant special blest,

By new unfolding his imprisoned pride.

    Blessed are you whose worthiness gives scope,

    Being had, to triumph, being lacked, to hope.

*Sonnet No 52*

THAT·IS·YOUR·SUBSTANCE, whereof are you made,
That millions of strange shadows on you tend?
Since every one hath, every one, one shade,
And you, but one, can every shadow lend.
Describe Adonis, and the counterfeit
Is poorly imitated after you;
On Helen's cheek all art of beauty set,
And you in Grecian tires are painted new.
Speak of the spring and foison of the year;
The one doth shadow of your beauty show,
The other as your bounty doth appear,
And you in every blessèd shape we know.
    In all external grace you have some part,
    But you like none, none you, for constant heart.

Sonnet No 53

·HOW·MUCH·MORE doth beauty beauteous seem
By that sweet ornament which truth doth give'!
The'rose'looks fair, but fairer we'it deem
For that sweet odour which doth in it live'.
The'canker blooms have'full as deep a dye'
As the'perfumèd tincture'of the'roses,
Hang on such thorns and play as wantonly
When summer's breath their maskèd buds discloses:
But for their virtue'only is their show;
They live'unwooed and unrespected fade',
Die' to themselves. Sweet roses do not so,
Of their sweet deaths are sweetest odours made':
   And so of you, beauteous and lovely youth,
   When that shall vade', my verse distils your truth.

Sonnet No 54

NOT·MARBLE nor the gilded monuments
Of princes shall outlive this powerful rhyme,
But you shall shine more bright in these contents
Than unswept stone, besmeared with sluttish time.
When wasteful war shall statues overturn,
And broils root out the work of masonry,
Nor Mars his sword nor war's quick fire shall burn
The living record of your memory.
'Gainst death and all oblivious enmity
Shall you pace forth; your praise shall still find room
Even in the eyes of all posterity
That wear this world out to the ending doom.
    So, till the judgement that yourself arise,
    You live in this, and dwell in lovers' eyes.

Sonnet No 55

SWEET·LOVE, renew thy force'; be'it not said
Thy edge'should blunter be'than appetite,'
Which but today by feeding is allayed,
Tomorrow sharpened in his former might.
So, love,' be'thou; although today thou fill
Thy hungry eyes even till they wink with fullness,
Tomorrow see again, and do not kill
The'spirit of love'with a perpetual dullness.
Let this sad interim like'the'ocean be'
Which parts the'shore' where'two contracted new
Come' daily to the'banks, that, when they see'
Return of love,' more'blest may be'the'view;

As call it winter, which being full of care'
Makes summer's welcome'thrice more'wished, more'rare'.

Sonnet No 56

**B**EING·YOUR·SLAVE, what should I do but tend
Upon the hours and times of your desire?
I have no precious time at all to spend,
Nor services to do, till you require.
Nor dare I chide the world-without-end hour
Whilst I, my sovereign, watch the clock for you,
Nor think the bitterness of absence sour
When you have bid your servant once adieu.
Nor dare I question with my jealous thought
Where you may be, or your affairs suppose,
But like a sad slave stay and think of naught
Save where you are how happy you make those.
So true a fool is love that, in your will
Though you do anything, he thinks no ill.

Sonnet No 57

HAT·GOD·FORBID that made me first your slave
  I should in thought control your times of pleasure,
  Or at your hand th'account of hours to crave,
Being your vassal bound to stay your leisure.
O, let me suffer, being at your beck,
Th'imprisoned absence of your liberty,
And, patience-tame to sufferance, bide each check
Without accusing you of injury.
Be where you list, your charter is so strong
That you yourself may privilege your time
To what you will; to you it doth belong
Yourself to pardon of self-doing crime.
  I am to wait, though waiting so be hell,
  Not blame your pleasure, be it ill or well.

Sonnet No 58

IF THERE·BE·NOTHING·NEW, but that which is
Hath been before, how are our brains beguiled,
Which, labouring for invention, bear amiss
The second burden of a former child !
O that record could with a backward look
Even of five hundred courses of the sun
Show me your image in some antique book,
Since mind at first in character was done,
That I might see what the old world could say
To this composèd wonder of your frame;
Whether we are mended, or whe'er better they,
Or whether revolution be the same.
O, sure I am the wits of former days
To subjects worse have given admiring praise.

Sonnet No 59

LIKE·AS·THE·WAVES make towards the pebbled shore
So do our minutes hasten to their end;
Each changing place with that which goes before,
In sequent toil all forwards do contend.
Nativity, once in the main of light,
Crawls to maturity, wherewith being crowned,
Crooked eclipses 'gainst his glory fight,
And Time that gave doth now his gift confound.
Time doth transfix the flourish set on youth,
And delves the parallels in beauty's brow,
Feeds on the rarities of nature's truth,
And nothing stands but for his scythe to mow.
  And yet to times in hope my verse shall stand,
  Praising thy worth, despite his cruel hand.

Sonnet No 60

IS IT·THY·WILL thy image should keep open
My heavy eyelids to the weary night?
Dost thou desire my slumbers should be broken,
While shadows like to thee do mock my sight?
Is it thy spirit that thou send'st from thee
So far from home into my deeds to pry,
To find out shames and idle hours in me,
The scope and tenour of thy jealousy?
Oh no! Thy love though much is not so great;
It is my love that keeps mine eye awake,
Mine own true love that doth my rest defeat,
To play the watchman ever for thy sake.
　　For thee watch I, whilst thou dost wake elsewhere,
　　From me far off, with others all too near.

Sonnet No 61

SIN·OF·self-love possesseth all mine eye,
And all my soul, and all my every part;
And for this sin there is no remedy,
It is so grounded inward in my heart.
Methinks no face so gracious is as mine,
No shape so true, no truth of such account,
And for myself mine own worth do define,
As I all other in all worths surmount.
But when my glass shows me my self indeed,
Beated and chopped with tanned antiquity,
Mine own self-love quite contrary I read—
Self so self-loving were iniquity:
'Tis thee (my self) that for myself I praise,
Painting my age with beauty of thy days.

Sonnet No 62

AGAINST · MY · LOVE shall be'as I am now,
With Time's injurious hand crushed and o'erworn,
When hours have'drained his blood and filled his brow
With lines and wrinkles; when his youthful morn
Hath travelled on to age's steepy night,
And all those'beauties whereof now he's king
Are'vanishing or vanished out of sight,
Stealing away the treasure'of his spring:
For such a time'do I now fortify
Against confounding age's cruel knife,
That he shall never cut from memory
My sweet love's beauty, though my lover's life:
His beauty shall in these black lines be'seen,
And they shall live, and he in them still green.

Sonnet No 63

WHEN I have seen by Time's fell hand defaced
The rich proud cost of outworn buried age;
When sometime lofty towers I see down razed,
And brass eternal slave to mortal rage;
When I have seen the hungry ocean gain
Advantage on the kingdom of the shore,
And the firm soil win of the watery main,
Increasing store with loss and loss with store;
When I have seen such interchange of state,
Or state itself confounded to decay,
Ruin hath taught me thus to ruminate:
That Time will come and take my love away.
  This thought is as a death, which cannot choose
  But weep to have that which it fears to lose.

Sonnet No 64

SINCE brass, nor stone, nor earth, nor boundless sea,
  But sad mortality o'ersways their power,
  How with this rage shall beauty hold a plea,
Whose action is no stronger than a flower?
O how shall summer's honey breath hold out
Against the wrackful siege of battering days,
When rocks impregnable are not so stout,
Nor gates of steel so strong, but Time decays?
O fearful meditation! Where, alack,
Shall Time's best jewel from Time's chest lie hid?
Or what strong hand can hold his swift foot back,
Or who his spoil of beauty can forbid?
    O none, unless this miracle have might:
    That in black ink my love may still shine bright.

Sonnet No 65

TIRED with all these' for restful death I cry:
As to behold Desert a beggar born,
And needy Nothing trimmed in jollity,
And purest Faith unhappily forsworn,
And gilded Honour shamefully misplaced,
And maiden Virtue' rudely strumpeted,
And right Perfection wrongfully disgraced,
And Strength by limping Sway disabled,
And Art made' tongue'- tied by Authority,
And Folly, Doctor-like', controlling Skill,
And simple' Truth miscalled Simplicity,
And captive Good attending captain Ill.
  Tired with all these', from these would I be' gone'—
  Save' that, to die', I leave' my love' alone.'

Sonnet No 66

AH; WHEREFORE with infection should he live'
And with his presence'grace'impiety
That sin by him advantage should achieve'
And lace'itself with his society ?
Why should false'painting imitate'his cheek
And steal dead seeming of his living hue'?
Why should poor beauty indirectly seek
Roses of shadow, since his rose'is true'?
Why should he'live', now Nature bankrupt is —
Beggared of blood to blush through lively veins,
For she'hath no exchequer now but his,
And proud of many, lives upon his gains ?
  Oh him she stores, to show what wealth she had
  In days long since', before'these last so bad.

Sonnet No 67

THUS·IS·HIS·CHEEK the map of days outworn
  When beauty lived and died as flowers do now,
    Before these bastard signs of fair were borne
Or durst inhabit on a living brow;
Before the golden tresses of the dead,
The right of sepulchres, were shorn away
To live a second life on second head;
Ere beauty's dead fleece made another gay.
In him those holy antique hours are seen
Without all ornament, itself and true,
Making no summer of another's green,
Robbing no old to dress his beauty new;
    And him as for a map doth Nature store,
    To show false Art what beauty was of yore.

Sonnet No 68

THOSE·PARTS of thee' that the' world's eye doth view
Want nothing that the' thought of hearts can mend;
    All tongues, the' voice' of souls, give' thee that due'
Uttering bare truth, even so as foes commend.
Thy outward thus with outward praise' is crowned,
But those' same' tongues that give' thee' so thine' own,
In other accents do this praise' confound
By seeing farther than the eye hath shown.
They look into the' beauty of thy mind,
And that in guess they measure by thy deeds;
Then churls their thoughts, although their eyes were' kind,
To thy fair flower add the' rank smell of weeds.
    But why thy odour matcheth not thy show,
    The soil is this, that thou dost common grow.

Sonnet No 69

THAT·THOU· art blamed shall not be thy defect,
　　For slander's mark was ever yet the fair;
　　The ornament of beauty is suspect,
A crow that flies in heaven's sweetest air.
So thou be good, slander doth but approve
Thy worth the greater, being wooed of time,
For canker vice the sweetest buds doth love,
And thou present'st a pure unstained prime.
Thou hast passed by the ambush of young days
Either not assailed, or victor being charged,
Yet this thy praise cannot be so thy praise
To tie up envy, evermore enlarged:
　　If some suspect of ill masked not thy show
　　Then thou alone kingdoms of hearts shouldst owe.

Sonnet No 70

NO·LONGER mourn for me when I am dead
Than you shall hear the surly sullen bell
Give warning to the world that I am fled
From this vile world with vilest worms to dwell:
Nay, if you read this line, remember not
The hand that writ it, for I love you so
That I in your sweet thoughts would be forgot
If thinking on me then should make you woe.
O if, I say, you look upon this verse
When I perhaps compounded am with clay,
Do not so much as my poor name rehearse
But let your love even with my life decay:
    Lest the wise world should look into your moan,
    And mock you with me after I am gone.

Sonnet No 71

·LEST·THE·WORLD should task you to recite'
What merit lived in me' that you should love',
After my death, dear love, forget me' quite',
For you in me' can nothing worthy prove',
Unless you would devise' some' virtuous lie'
To do more for me' than mine' own desert',
And hang more' praise' upon deceasèd I
Than niggard truth would willingly impart.
O lest your true love may seem false' in this,
That you for love speak well of me untrue',
My name' be' buried where my body is,
And live no more to shame' nor me' nor you :

    For I am shamed by that which I bring forth,
    And so should you, to love things nothing worth.

Sonnet No 72

THAT·TIME·OF·YEAR thou mayst in me behold
When yellow leaves, or none, or few, do hang
Upon those' boughs which shake' against the cold,
Bare' ruined choirs where late' the' sweet birds sang.
In me' thou seest the' twilight of such day,
As after sunset fadeth in the' west,
Which by and by black night doth take' away,
Death's second self that seals up all in rest.
In me thou seest the glowing of such fire,'
That on the' ashes of his youth doth lie,'
As the' death-bed whereon it must expire,'
Consumed with that which it was nourished by.
  Thus thou perceiv'st, which makes thy love more strong,
  To love that well, which thou must leave' ere long.

Sonnet No 73

BUT BE CONTENTED, when that fell arrest
Without all bail shall carry me away,
My life hath in this line some interest,
Which for memorial still with thee shall stay.
When thou reviewest this, thou dost review
The very part was consecrate to thee;
The earth can have but earth, which is his due,
My spirit is thine, the better part of me.
So then thou hast but lost the dregs of life,
The prey of worms, my body being dead,
The coward conquest of a wretch's knife,
Too base of thee to be remembered.
    The worth of that, is that which it contains,
    And that is this, and this with thee remains.

Sonnet No 74

SO·ARE·YOU to my thoughts as food to life,
    Or as sweet seasoned showers are to the ground;
    And for the peace of you I hold such strife
As 'twixt a miser and his wealth is found:
Now proud as an enjoyer, and anon
Doubting the filching age will steal his treasure;
Now counting best to be with you alone,
Then bettered that the world may see my pleasure;
Sometime all full with feasting on your sight,
And by and by clean starvèd for a look;
Possessing or pursuing no delight
Save what is had, or must from you be took.
    Thus do I pine and surfeit day by day,
    Or gluttoning on all, or all away.

Sonnet No 75

WHY IS MY VERSE so barren of new pride,
So far from variation or quick change?
Why with the time do I not glance aside
To new-found methods and to compounds strange?
Why write I still all one, ever the same,
And keep invention in a noted weed,
That every word doth almost tell my name,
Showing their birth and where they did proceed?
O know, sweet love, I always write of you,
And you and love are still my argument:
So all my best is dressing old words new,
Spending again what is already spent:
    For as the sun is daily new and old,
    So is my love still telling what is told.

Sonnet No 76

THY·GLASS WILL SHOW thee how thy beauties wear,
Thy dial how thy precious minutes waste,
The vacant leaves thy mind's imprint will bear,
And of this book this learning mayst thou taste:
The wrinkles which thy glass will truly show
Of mouthed graves will give thee memory:
Thou by thy dial's shady stealth mayst know
Time's thievish progress to eternity.
Look what thy memory cannot contain
Commit to these waste blanks and thou shalt find
Those children nursed, delivered from thy brain,
To take a new acquaintance of thy mind.
  These offices, so oft as thou wilt look,
  Shall profit thee and much enrich thy book.

Sonnet No 77

SO·OFT·HAVE· I invoked thee for my Muse
    And found such fair assistance in my verse
    As every alien pen hath got my use
And under thee their poesy disperse.
Thine eyes, that taught the dumb on high to sing,
And heavy ignorance aloft to fly,
Have added feathers to the learnèd's wing,
And given grace a double majesty.
Yet be most proud of that which I compile,
Whose influence is thine, and born of thee,
In others' works thou dost but mend the style,
And arts with thy sweet graces gracèd be.
    But thou art all my art, and dost advance
    As high as learning, my rude ignorance.

Sonnet No 78

WHILST·I·ALONE did call upon thy aid,
   My verse alone had all thy gentle grace,
      But now my gracious numbers are decayed,
And my sick Muse doth give another place.
   I grant, sweet love, thy lovely argument
Deserves the travail of a worthier pen,
Yet what of thee thy Poet doth invent,
He robs thee of, and pays it thee again:
He lends thee virtue, and he stole that word,
From thy behaviour; beauty doth he give,
And found it in thy cheek; he can afford
No praise to thee, but what in thee doth live.
      Then thank him not for that which he doth say,
      Since what he owes thee, thou thyself dost pay.

Sonnet No 79

HOW·I·FAINT· when I of you do write,
Knowing a better spirit doth use your name,
And in the praise thereof spends all his might,
To make me tongue- tied speaking of your fame!
But since your worth, wide as the ocean is,
The humble as the proudest sail doth bear,
My saucy bark, inferior far to his,
On your broad main doth wilfully appear.
Your shallowest help will hold me up afloat,
Whilst he upon your soundless deep doth ride;
Or being wrecked, I am a worthless boat,
He of tall building and of goodly pride.
    Then if he thrive and I be cast away
    The worst was this : my love was my decay.

Sonnet No 80

OR·I·SHALL·LIVE your epitaph to make,
Or you survive when I in earth am rotten,
    From hence your memory death cannot take,
Although in me each part will be forgotten.
Your name from hence immortal life shall have
Though I, once gone, to all the world must die;
The earth can yield me but a common grave,
When you entombèd in men's eyes shall lie.
Your monument shall be my gentle verse,
Which eyes not yet created shall o'er-read,
And tongues to be your being shall rehearse
When all the breathers of this world are dead:
    You still shall live — such virtue hath my pen —
    Where breath most breathes, even in the mouths of men.

Sonnet No 81

I GRANT thou wert not married to my Muse,
And therefore mayst without attaint o'erlook
The dedicated words which writers use
Of their fair subject, blessing every book.
Thou art as fair in knowledge as in hue,
Finding thy worth a limit past my praise,
And therefore art enforced to seek anew,
Some fresher stamp of the time-bettering days.
And do so love; yet when they have devised
What strained touches rhetoric can lend,
Thou, truly fair, wert truly sympathized
In true plain words by thy true-telling friend.
    And their gross painting might be better used
    Where cheeks need blood; in thee it is abused.

Sonnet No 82

I NEVER·SAW that you did painting need,
    And therefore to your fair no painting set;
    I found, or thought I found, you did exceed
The barren tender of a poet's debt:
And therefore have I slept in your report,
That you yourself being extant well might show
How far a modern quill doth come too short,
Speaking of worth, what worth in you doth grow.
This silence for my sin you did impute,
Which shall be most my glory being dumb;
For I impair not beauty, being mute,
When others would give life, and bring a tomb:
        There lives more life in one of your fair eyes
        Than both your poets can in praise devise.

Sonnet No 83

WHO·IS·IT that says most, which can say more,
Than this rich praise, that you alone are you,
In whose confine immurèd is the store
Which should example where your equal grew?
Lean penury within that pen doth dwell
That to his subject lends not some small glory,
But he that writes of you, if he can tell,
That you are you, so dignifies his story.
Let him but copy what in you is writ,
Not making worse what nature made so clear,
And such a counterpart shall fame his wit,
Making his style admirèd every where.

     You to your beauteous blessings add a curse,
     Being fond on praise, which makes your praises worse.

Sonnet No 84

MY·TONGUE·Tied Muse in manners holds her still
While comments of your praise, richly compiled,
Reserve their character with golden quill
And precious phrase by all the Muses filed.
I think good thoughts, whilst others write good words,
And like unlettered clerk still cry Amen,
To every hymn that able spirit affords
In polished form of well-refinèd pen.
Hearing you praised I say, 'Tis so, 'tis true,'
And to the most of praise add something more';
But that is in my thought, whose love to you,
Though words come hindmost, holds his rank before.
    Then others, for the breath of words respect,
    Me for my dumb thoughts, speaking in effect.

Sonnet No 85

WAS·IT the proud full sail of his great verse,
  Bound for the prize of all-too-precious you,
  That did my ripe thoughts in my brain inhearse,
Making their tomb the womb wherein they grew?
Was it his spirit, by spirits taught to write,
Above a mortal pitch, that struck me dead?
No, neither he, nor his compeers by night
Giving him aid, my verse astonishèd:
He, nor that affable familiar ghost
Which nightly gulls him with intelligence,
As victors of my silence cannot boast;
I was not sick of any fear from thence.
    But when your countenance filled up his line,
    Then lacked I matter, that enfeebled mine.

Sonnet No 86

FAREWELL – thou art too dear for my possessing,
    And like enough thou know'st thy estimate.
    The charter of thy worth gives thee releasing,
My bonds in thee are all determinate.
For how do I hold thee but by thy granting
And for that riches where is my deserving?
The cause of this fair gift in me is wanting,
And so my patent back again is swerving.
Thyself thou gav'st, thy own worth then not knowing,
Or me, to whom thou gav'st it, else mistaking:
So thy great gift, upon misprision growing,
Comes home again on better judgement making.
    Thus have I had thee as a dream doth flatter –
    In sleep a king, but waking no such matter.

Sonnet No 87

WHEN·THOU shalt be disposed to set me light
And place my merit in the eye of scorn,
Upon thy side against myself I'll fight,
And prove thee virtuous, though thou art forsworn.
With mine own weakness being best acquainted,
Upon thy part I can set down a story
Of faults concealed wherein I am attainted,
That thou in losing me shall win much glory:
And I by this will be a gainer too,
For bending all my loving thoughts on thee
The injuries that to myself I do,
Doing thee vantage, double vantage me.
    Such is my love, to thee I so belong,
    That for thy right, myself will bear all wrong.

Sonnet No 88

SAY·THAT thou didst forsake me for some fault,
  And I will comment upon that offence;
    Speak of my lameness, and I straight will halt,
Against thy reasons making no defence.
Thou canst not, love, disgrace me half so ill,
To set a form upon desired change,
As I'll myself disgrace; knowing thy will,
I will acquaintance strangle and look strange,
Be absent from thy walks, and in my tongue
Thy sweet beloved name no more shall dwell,
Lest I, too much profane, should do it wrong
And haply of our old acquaintance tell.
    For thee, against my self I'll vow debate,
    For I must ne'er love him whom thou dost hate.

Sonnet No 89

THEN·HATE·ME when thou wilt - if ever, now:
Now, while the world is bent my deeds to cross,
Join with the spite of Fortune, make me bow,
And do not drop in for an after-loss.
Ah do not, when my heart hath 'scaped this sorrow,
Come in the rearward of a conquered woe;
Give not a windy night a rainy morrow,
To linger out a purposed overthrow.
If thou wilt leave me, do not leave me last,
When other petty griefs have done their spite,
But in the onset come: so shall I taste
At first the very worst of Fortune's might;
And other strains of woe, which now seem woe,
Compared with loss of thee will not seem so.

*Sonnet No 90*

SOME·GLORY in their birth, some in their skill,
Some in their wealth, some in their body's force,
Some in their garments, though new-fangled ill,
Some in their hawks and hounds, some in their horse:
And every humour hath his adjunct pleasure
Wherein it finds a joy above the rest;
But these particulars are not my measure:
All these I better in one general best.
Thy love is better than high birth to me,
Richer than wealth, prouder than garments' cost,
Of more delight than hawks or horses be;
And having thee, of all men's pride I boast,
  Wretched in this alone: that thou mayst take
  All this away and me most wretched make.

Sonnet No 91

BUT·DO·THY·WORST to steal thyself away,
  For term of life thou art assurèd mine,
  And life no longer than thy love will stay,
For it depends upon that love of thine.
Then need I not to fear the worst of wrongs,
When in the least of them my life hath end;
I see a better state to me belongs
Than that which on thy humour doth depend.
Thou canst not vex me with inconstant mind,
Since that my life on thy revolt doth lie:
Oh, what a happy title do I find—
Happy to have thy love, happy to die!
    But what's so blessed fair that fears no blot?
    Thou mayst be false, and yet I know it not.

Sonnet No 92

SO·SHALL·I·LIVE supposing thou art true,
Like a deceivèd husband; so love's face
May still seem love to me, though altered new~
Thy looks with me, thy heart in other place;
For there can live no hatred in thine eye,
Therefore in that I cannot know thy change.
In many's looks the false heart's history
Is writ in moods and frowns and wrinkles strange,
But heaven in thy creation did decree
That in thy face sweet love should ever dwell;
Whate'er thy thoughts or thy heart's workings be,
Thy looks should nothing thence but sweetness tell.
    How like Eve's apple doth thy beauty grow
    If thy sweet virtue answer not thy show!

Sonnet No 93

THEY·THAT·HAVE POWER to hurt & will do none,
That do not do the thing they most do show,
Who, moving others, are themselves as stone
Unmovèd, cold, and to temptation slow:
They rightly do inherit heaven's graces
And husband nature's riches from expense;
They are the lords and owners of their faces,
Others but stewards of their excellence.
The summer's flower is to the summer sweet,
Though to itself it only live and die;
But if that flower with base infection meet,
The basest weed outbraves his dignity:

    For sweetest things turn sourest by their deeds;
    Lilies that fester smell far worse than weeds.

Sonnet No 94

HOW·SWEET and lovely dost thou make the shame
Which like a canker in the fragrant rose
Doth spot the beauty of thy budding name—
Oh, in what sweets dost thou thy sins enclose!
That tongue that tells the story of thy days,
Making lascivious comments on thy sport,
Cannot dispraise, but in a kind of praise,
Naming thy name, blesses an ill report.
Oh, what a mansion have those vices got
Which for their habitation chose out thee—
Where beauty's veil doth cover every blot
And all things turns to fair that eyes can see!
Take heed, dear heart, of this large privilege;
The hardest knife ill used doth lose his edge.

Sonnet No 95

SOME·SAY thy fault is youth, some wantonness;
Some say thy grace is youth and gentle sport;
Both grace and faults are loved of more and less:
Thou mak'st faults graces that to thee resort.
As on the finger of a thronèd queen
The basest jewel will be well esteemed,
So are those errors that in thee are seen
To truths translated and for true things deemed.
How many lambs might the stern wolf betray
If like a lamb he could his looks translate!
How many gazers mightst thou lead away
If thou wouldst use the strength of all thy state!
  But do not so, I love thee in such sort
  As, thou being mine, mine is thy good report.

Sonnet No 96

OW·LIKE·A·WINTER hath my absence been
From thee, the pleasure of the fleeting year;
What freezings have I felt, what dark days seen,
What old December's bareness everywhere!
And yet this time removed was summer's time,
The teeming autumn big with rich increase,
Bearing the wanton burthen of the prime
Like widowed wombs after their lords' decease:
Yet this abundant issue seemed to me
But hope of orphans and unfathered fruit
For Summer and his pleasures wait on thee,
And, thou away, the very birds are mute:
        Or if they sing, 'tis with so dull a cheer
        That leaves look pale, dreading the winter's near.

Sonnet No 97

FROM·YOU have I been absent in the spring,
When proud-pied April, dressed in all his trim,
  Hath put a spirit of youth in everything,
That heavy Saturn laughed and leapt with him.
Yet nor the lays of birds, nor the sweet smell
Of different flowers in odour and in hue,
Could make me any summer's story tell,
Or from their proud lap pluck them where they grew:
Nor did I wonder at the lily's white,
Nor praise the deep vermilion in the rose;
They were but sweet, but figures of delight
Drawn after you, you pattern of all those.
    Yet seemed it winter still; and, you away,
    As with your shadow I with these did play.

Sonnet No 98

THE·FORWARD violet thus did I chide':
'Sweet thief, whence' didst thou steal thy sweet that smells,
If not from my love's breath? The'purple'pride'
Which on thy soft cheek for complexion dwells
In my love's veins thou hast too grossly dyed.'
The'lily I condemnèd for thy hand,
And buds of marjoram had stol'n thy hair;
The'roses fearfully on thorns did stand—
One blushing shame', another white'despair;
A third, nor red nor white', had stol'n of both,
And to his robbery had annexed thy breath,
But for his theft in pride'of all his growth
A vengeful canker eat him up to death.

More flowers I noted, yet I none could see'
But sweet or colour it had stol'n from thee'.

Sonnet No 99

WHERE art thou, Muse, that thou forget'st so long
To speak of that which gives thee all thy might?
Spend'st thou thy fury on some worthless song,
Darkening thy power to lend base subjects light?
Return forgetful Muse, and straight redeem,
In gentle numbers time so idly spent,
Sing to the ear that doth thy lays esteem,
And gives thy pen both skill and argument.
Rise resty Muse, my love's sweet face survey,
If time have any wrinkle graven there,
If any, be a satire to decay,
And make Time's spoils despised every where.
Give my love fame faster than time wastes life,
So thou prevent'st his scythe, and crooked knife.

Sonnet No 100

· TRUANT · MUSE, what shall be thy amends
For thy neglect of truth in beauty dyed?
    Both truth and beauty on my love depends;
So dost thou too, and therein dignified.
Make answer, Muse! Wilt thou not haply say
'Truth needs no colour with his colour fixed,
Beauty no pencil, beauty's truth to lay;
But best is best if never intermixed?'
Because he needs no praise, wilt thou be dumb?
Excuse not silence so, for't lies in thee
To make him much outlive a gilded tomb,
And to be praised of ages yet to be.
    Then do thy office, Muse; I teach thee how
    To make him seem, long hence, as he shows now.

Y LOVE is strengthened, though more weak in seeming;
I love not less, though less the show appear,
That love is merchandized whose rich esteeming
The owner's tongue doth publish everywhere.
Our love was new, and then but in the spring,
When I was wont to greet it with my lays,
As Philomel in summer's front doth sing,
And stops her pipe in growth of riper days:
Not that the summer is less pleasant now
Than when her mournful hymns did hush the night,
But that wild music burthens every bough,
And sweets grown common lose their dear delight.
    Therefore like her, I sometime hold my tongue,
    Because I would not dull you with my song.

Sonnet No 102

ALACK, what poverty my Muse brings forth,
  That having such a scope to show her pride
  The argument all bare is of more worth
Than when it hath my added praise beside!
O, blame me not if I no more can write;
Look in your glass, and there appears a face
That overgoes my blunt invention quite,
Dulling my lines and doing me disgrace.
Were it not sinful then, striving to mend,
To mar the subject that before was well?
For to no other pass my verses tend
Than of your graces and your gifts to tell:
    And more, much more, than in my verse can sit
    Your own glass shows you when you look in it.

Sonnet No 103

TO·ME, FAIR·FRIEND, you never can be'old;
  For as you were'when first your eye'I eyed,
  Such seems your beauty still. Three'winters cold
Have'from the'forests shook three'summers'pride,
Three'beauteous springs to yellow autumn turned;
In process of the'seasons have'I seen
Three'April perfumes in three hot Junes burned,
Since'first I saw you fresh which yet are'green.
Ah, yet doth beauty like'a dial hand
  Steal from his figure', and no pace'perceived,
So your sweet hue', which methinks still doth stand,
Hath motion, and mine'eye may be deceived:
  For fear of which hear this, thou age unbred,
  Ere you were'born was beauty's summer dead.

Sonnet No 104

LET·NOT·MY·LOVE be called idolatry,
Nor my beloved as an idol show,
Since all alike my songs and praises be
To one, of one, still such, and ever so.
Kind is my love today, tomorrow kind,
Still constant in a wondrous excellence:
Therefore my verse, to constancy confined,
One thing expressing, leaves out difference.
'Fair, kind, and true' is all my argument:
'Fair, kind, and true' varying to other words;
And in this change is my invention spent,
Three themes in one, which wondrous scope affords.
    Fair, kind, and true have often lived alone,
    Which three till now never kept seat in one.

WHEN·IN·THE·CHRONICLE of wasted time
I see descriptions of the fairest wights,
And beauty making beautiful old rhyme
In praise of ladies dead and lovely knights,
Then in the blazon of sweet beauty's best —
Of hand, of foot, of lip, of eye, of brow —
I see their antique pen would have expressed
Even such a beauty as you master now.
So all their praises are but prophecies
Of this our time, all you prefiguring,
And, for they looked but with divining eyes,
They had not skill enough your worth to sing:
    For we, which now behold these present days,
    Have eyes to wonder, but lack tongues to praise.

Sonnet No 106

NOT·MINE own fears nor the prophetic soul
Of the wide world, dreaming on things to come,
Can yet the lease of my true love control,
Supposed as forfeit to a confined doom.
The mortal moon hath her eclipse endured,
And the sad augurs mock their own presage,
Incertainties now crown themselves assured,
And peace proclaims olives of endless age.
Now with the drops of this most balmy time
My love looks fresh, and Death to me subscribes,
Since, spite of him, I'll live in this poor rhyme,
While he insults o'er dull and speechless tribes:
    And thou in this shalt find thy monument
    When tyrants' crests and tombs of brass are spent.

Sonnet No 107

WHAT'S·IN·THE·BRAIN that ink may character,
Which hath not figured to thee my true spirit?
What's new to speak, what now to register,
That may express my love, or thy dear merit?
Nothing, sweet boy, but yet like prayers divine
I must each day say o'er the very same,
Counting no old thing old — thou mine, I thine —
Even as when first I hallowed thy fair name.
So that eternal love in love's fresh case
Weighs not the dust and injury of age,
Nor gives to necessary wrinkles place,
But makes antiquity for aye his page,
     Finding the first conceit of love there bred
     Where time and outward form would show it dead.

Sonnet No 108

O NEVER·SAY that I was false of heart,
Though absence seemed my flame to qualify;
As easy might I from my self depart
As from my soul, which in thy breast doth lie:
That is my home of love; if I have ranged,
Like him that travels I return again,
Just to the time, not with the time exchanged,
So that myself bring water for my stain.
Never believe, though in my nature reigned
All frailties that besiege all kinds of blood,
That it could so preposterously be stained
To leave for nothing all thy sum of good:
    For nothing this wide universe I call
    Save thou, my rose; in it thou art my all.

Sonnet No 109

ALAS ·'TIS·TRUE, I have gone here and there
    And made myself a motley to the view;
    Gored mine own thoughts, sold cheap what is most dear,
Made old offences of affections new.
Most true it is that I have looked on truth
Askance and strangely: but by all above,
These blenches gave my heart another youth,
And worse essays proved thee my best of love.
Now all is done, have what shall have no end;
Mine appetite I never more will grind
On newer proof to try an older friend—
A god in love, to whom I am confined.
        Then give me welcome, next my heaven the best,
        Even to thy pure and most most loving breast.

Sonnet No 110

FOR·MY·SAKE do you with Fortune chide,
The guilty goddess of my harmful deeds,
That did not better for my life provide
Than public means which public manners breeds.
Thence comes it that my name receives a brand,
And almost thence my nature is subdued
To what it works in, like the dyer's hand.
Pity me then, and wish I were renewed,
Whilst like a willing patient I will drink
Potions of eisel 'gainst my strong infection,
No bitterness that I will bitter think,
Nor double penance to correct correction.
    Pity me then, dear friend, and I assure ye
    Even that your pity is enough to cure me.

Sonnet No 111

YOUR·LOVE and pity doth the impression fill
Which vulgar scandal stamped upon my brow;
For what care'I who calls me'well or ill,
So you o'ergreen my bad, my good allow?
You are'my all the'world, and I must strive'
To know my shames and praises from your tongue';
None'else' to me', nor I to none'alive,
That my steeled sense'or changes right or wrong.
In so profound abysm I throw all care'
Of others' voices, that my adder's sense'
To critic and to flatterer stoppèd are'.
Mark how with my neglect I do dispense':
     You are so strongly in my purpose' bred
     That all the world besides methinks are dead.

Sonnet No 112

SINCE·I·LEFT·YOU, mine eye is in my mind.
   And that which governs me to go about
      Doth part his function and is partly blind,
Seems seeing, but effectually is out:
For it no form delivers to the heart
Of bird, of flower, or shape which it doth latch;
Of his quick objects hath the mind no part,
Nor his own vision holds what it doth catch:
For if it see the rud'st or gentlest sight,
The most sweet favour, or deformèd'st creature,
The mountain, or the sea, the day, or night,
The crow, or dove, it shapes them to your feature:
      Incapable of more, replete with you,
         My most true mind thus maketh mine eye untrue.

Sonnet No 113

· WHETHER doth my mind, being crowned with you,
Drink up the monarch's plague, this flattery,
Or whether shall I say mine eye saith true,
And that your love taught it this alchemy:
To make of monsters and things indigest
Such cherubins as your sweet self resemble,
Creating every bad a perfect best
As fast as objects to his beams assemble?
Oh, 'tis the first — 'tis flattery in my seeing,
And my great mind most kingly drinks it up;
Mine eye well knows what with his gust is 'greeing,
And to his palate doth prepare the cup.
    If it be poisoned, 'tis the lesser sin
    That mine eye loves it and doth first begin.

Sonnet No 114

THOSE·LINES that I before have writ do lie,
Even those that said I could not love you dearer,
Yet then my judgement knew no reason why
My most full flame should afterwards burn clearer.
But reckoning Time, whose millioned accidents
Creep in 'twixt vows, and change decrees of kings,
Tan sacred beauty, blunt the sharp'st intents,
Divert strong minds to the course of altering things:
Alas, why, fearing of Time's tyranny,
Might I not then say, 'Now I love you best,'
When I was certain o'er incertainty,
Crowning the present, doubting of the rest?
    Love is a babe: then might I not say so,
    To give full growth to that which still doth grow.

Sonnet No 115

LET ME NOT to the marriage of true minds
Admit impediments; love is not love
Which alters when it alteration finds,
Or bends with the remover to remove.
O no, it is an ever-fixèd mark
That looks on tempests and is never shaken;
It is the star to every wandering bark,
Whose worth's unknown, although his height be taken.
Love's not Time's fool, though rosy lips and cheeks
Within his bending sickle's compass come;
Love alters not with his brief hours and weeks,
But bears it out even to the edge of doom.
   If this be error and upon me proved,
   I never writ, nor no man ever loved.

Sonnet No 116

ACCUSE·ME·THUS: that I have scanted all
Wherein I should your great deserts repay,
Forgot upon your dearest love to call,
Whereto all bonds do tie me day by day;
That I have frequent been with unknown minds,
And given to time your own dear-purchased right,
That I have hoisted sail to all the winds
Which should transport me farthest from your sight.
Book both my wilfulness and errors down,
And on just proof surmise accumulate:
Bring me within the level of your frown,
But shoot not at me in your wakened hate:
 Since my appeal says I did strive to prove
 The constancy and virtue of your love.

Sonnet No 117

LIKE·AS·TO·MAKE our appetites more keen,
With eager compounds we our palate urge,
As to prevent our maladies unseen
We sicken to shun sickness when we purge,
Even so, being full of your ne'er cloying sweetness,
To bitter sauces did I frame my feeding;
And, sick of welfare, found a kind of meetness
To be diseased ere that there was true needing.
Thus policy in love, to anticipate
The ills that were not, grew to faults assured,
And brought to medicine a healthful state
Which, rank of goodness, would by ill be cured.
  But thence I learn, and find the lesson true,
  Drugs poison him that so fell sick of you.

Sonnet No 118

WHAT·POTIONS have I drunk of Siren tears
Distilled from limbecks foul as hell within,
Applying fears to hopes and hopes to fears,
Still losing when I saw myself to win!
What wretched errors hath my heart committed
Whilst it hath thought itself so blessèd never;
How have mine eyes out of their spheres been fitted
In the distraction of this madding fever!
O, benefit of ill! Now I find true
That better is by evil still made better,
And ruined love, when it is built anew
Grows fairer than at first, more strong, far greater.
　　So I return, rebuked, to my content,
　　And gain by ills thrice more than I have spent.

Sonnet No 119

THAT YOU were once unkind befriends me now,
And for that sorrow which I then did feel
Needs must I under my transgression bow,
Unless my nerves were brass or hammered steel.
For if you were by my unkindness shaken
As I by yours, you have passed a hell of time;
And I, a tyrant, have no leisure taken
To weigh how once I suffered in your crime.
O that our night of woe might have remembered
My deepest sense how hard true sorrow hits,
And soon to you, as you to me then, tendered
The humble salve which wounded bosoms fits!
But that your trespass now becomes a fee:
Mine ransoms yours, and yours must ransom me.

Sonnet No 120

'TIS·BETTER to be vile than vile esteemed,
When not to be receives reproach of being,
And the just pleasure lost which is so deemed
Not by our feeling, but by others' seeing.
For why should others' false adulterate eyes
Give salutation to my sportive blood?
Or on my frailties why are frailer spies,
Which in their wills count bad what I think good?
No, I am that I am, and they that level
At my abuses reckon up their own;
I may be straight though they themselves be bevel;
By their rank thoughts my deeds must not be shown,
Unless this general evil they maintain:
All men are bad and in their badness reign.

Sonnet No 121

THY·GIFT, thy tables, are within my brain
   Full charactered with lasting memory,
   Which shall above that idle rank remain
Beyond all date, even to eternity —
Or, at the least, so long as brain and heart
Have faculty by nature to subsist;
Till each to razed oblivion yield his part
Of thee, thy record never can be missed.
That poor retention could not so much hold,
Nor need I tallies thy dear love to score;
Therefore to give them from me was I bold,
To trust those tables that receive thee more.
      To keep an adjunct to remember thee
      Were to import forgetfulness in me.

Sonnet No 122

NO, TIME, thou shalt not boast that I do change:
The pyramids built up with newer might
To me are nothing novel, nothing strange,
They are but dressings of a former sight.
Our dates are brief, and therefore we admire
What thou dost foist upon us that is old,
And rather make them born to our desire
Than think that we before have heard them told.
Thy registers and thee I both defy,
Not wondering at the present, nor the past:
For thy records and what we see doth lie,
Made more or less by thy continual haste.
This I do vow and this shall ever be:
I will be true despite thy scythe and thee.

Sonnet No 123

**IF**·MY·DEAR·LOVE were but the child of state,
It might for Fortune's bastard be unfathered,
As subject to Time's love or to Time's hate,
Weeds among weeds or flowers with flowers gathered.
No it was builded far from accident;
It suffers not in smiling pomp, nor falls
Under the blow of thralled discontent
Whereto the inviting time our fashion calls;
It fears not policy, that heretic
Which works on leases of short-numbered hours,
But all alone stands hugely politic,
That it nor grows with heat nor drowns with showers.
        To this I witness call the fools of time,
        Which die for goodness, who have lived for crime.

Sonnet No 124

WERE·T·AUGHT to me I bore the canopy,
With my extern the outward honouring,
Or laid great bases for eternity
Which proves more short than waste or ruining?
Have I not seen dwellers on form and favour
Lose all, and more, by paying too much rent,
For compound sweet forgoing simple savour—
Pitiful thrivers in their gazing spent?
No, let me be obsequious in thy heart,
And take thou my oblation, poor but free,
Which is not mixed with seconds, knows no art
But mutual render, only me for thee.
    Hence, thou suborned informer! A true soul
    When most impeached stands least in thy control.

Sonnet No 125

THOU, MY·LOVELY·BOY, who in thy power
Dost hold Time's fickle glass, his sickle hour,
Who hast by waning grown, and therein show'st
Thy lovers withering as thy sweet self grow'st:
If Nature, sovereign mistress over wrack,
As thou goest onwards, still will pluck thee back,
She keeps thee to this purpose, that her skill
May Time disgrace and wretched minutes kill.
Yet fear her, O thou minion of her pleasure!
She may detain, but not still keep her treasure.
Her audit, though delayed, answered must be,
And her quietus is to render thee.

(                                        )
(                                        )

Sonnet No 126

**THE·OLD·AGE·BLACK** was not counted FAIR,

Or if it were it bore not beauty's name;

But now is black beauty's successive heir,

And beauty slandered with a bastard shame:

For since each hand hath put on Nature's power,

Fairing the foul with Art's false borrowed face,

Sweet Beauty hath no name, no holy bower,

But is profaned, if not lives in disgrace.

Therefore my mistress' eyes are raven black,

Her eyes so suited, and they mourners seem

At such who, not born fair, no beauty lack,

Slandering creation with a false esteem:

Yet so they mourn, becoming of their woe,

That every tongue says beauty should look so.

Sonnet No 127

HOW·OFT, when thou, my music, music play'st
Upon that blessed wood whose motion sounds
With thy sweet fingers, when thou gently sway'st
The' wiry concord that mine' ear confounds,
Do I envy those' jacks that nimble' leap
To kiss the' tender inward of thy hand,
Whilst my poor lips, which should that harvest reap,
At the' wood's boldness by thee blushing stand :
To be so tickled they would change' their state'
And situation with those' dancing chips
O'er whom thy fingers walk with gentle' gait,
Making dead wood more' blessed than living lips.

     Since' saucy jacks so happy are in this,
     Give them thy fingers, me' thy lips to kiss.

Sonnet No 128

THE·EXPENSE·OF·SPIRIT in a waste of shame
Is lust in action; and till action, lust
Is perjured, murderous, bloody, full of blame,
Savage, extreme, rude, cruel, not to trust,
Enjoyed no sooner but despisèd straight;
Past reason hunted and, no sooner had,
Past reason hated, as a swallowed bait
On purpose laid to make the taker mad —
Mad in pursuit, and in possession so;
Had, having, and in quest to have, extreme;
A bliss in proof, and proved, a very woe;
Before, a joy proposed; behind, a dream.
All this the world well knows, yet none knows well
To shun the heaven that leads men to this hell.

Sonnet No 129

MY·MISTRESS'·EYES are'nothing like'the'sun;
Coral is far more'red than her lips'red;
If snow be'white', why then her breasts are'dun;
If hairs be'wires, black wires grow on her head.
I have seen roses damasked, red and white',
But no such roses see' I in her cheeks,
And in some'perfumes is there'more'delight,
Than in the'breath that from my mistress reeks.
I love'to hear her speak, yet well I know,
That music hath a far more'pleasing sound:
I grant I never saw a goddess go—
My mistress when she'walks treads on the'ground.
    And yet, by heaven, I think my love'as rare'
    As any she'belied with false compare'.

Sonnet No 130

THOU·ART·AS·TYRANNOUS, so as thou art,
As those whose beauties proudly make them cruel;
For well thou know'st to my dear doting heart
Thou art the fairest and most precious jewel.
Yet in good faith some say, that thee behold,
Thy face hath not the power to make love groan;
To say they err I dare not be so bold,
Although I swear it to myself alone.
And to be sure that is not false I swear,
A thousand groans but thinking on thy face,
One on another's neck, do witness bear
Thy black is fairest in my judgement's place.
    In nothing art thou black save in thy deeds,
    And thence this slander as I think proceeds.

Sonnet No 131

THINE·EYES·I·LOVE, and they as pitying me,
Knowing thy heart torment me with disdain,
Have put on black, and loving mourners be,
Looking with pretty ruth upon my pain.
And truly not the morning sun of heaven
Better becomes the grey cheeks of the east,
Nor that full star that ushers in the even
Doth half that glory to the sober west
As those two mourning eyes become thy face.
O, let it then as well beseem thy heart
To mourn for me, since mourning doth thee grace,
And suit thy pity like in every part.
  Then will I swear beauty herself is black,
  And all they foul that thy complexion lack.

Sonnet No 132

BESHREW that heart that makes my heart to groan
For that deep wound it gives my friend and me!
Is't not enough to torture me alone,
But slave to slavery my sweet'st friend must be?
Me from myself thy cruel eye hath taken,
And my next self thou harder hast engrossed:
Of him, myself, and thee, I am forsaken —
A torment thrice threefold thus to be crossed.
Prison my heart in thy steel bosom's ward,
But then my friend's heart let my poor heart bail;
Whoe'er keeps me, let my heart be his guard:
Thou canst not then use rigour in my jail.
        And yet thou wilt, for I, being pent in thee,
            Perforce am thine, and all that is in me.

Sonnet No 133

SNOW·I·HAVE·CONFESSED that he is thine,
And I myself am mortgaged to thy will,
, Myself I'll forfeit, so that other mine
Thou wilt restore to be my comfort still.
But thou wilt not, nor he will not be free,
For thou art covetous, and he is kind;
He learned but surety-like to write for me
Under that bond that him as fast doth bind.
The statute of thy beauty thou wilt take,
Thou usurer, that putt'st forth all to use,
And sue a friend came debtor for my sake;
So him I lose through my unkind abuse.
    Him have I lost; thou hast both him and me;
    He pays the whole, and yet am I not free.

Sonnet No 134

WHOEVER·HATH·HER·WISH, thou hast thy Will,
And Will to boot, and Will in overplus:
More than enough am I that vex thee still,
To thy sweet will making addition thus.
Wilt thou, whose will is large and spacious,
Not once vouchsafe to hide my will in thine?
Shall will in others seem right gracious,
And in my will no fair acceptance shine?
The sea, all water, yet receives rain still,
And in abundance addeth to his store:
So thou being rich in Will add to thy Will
One will of mine to make thy large Will more.
    Let 'No', unkind, no fair beseechers kill;
    Think all but one, and me in that one Will.

Sonnet No 135

**IF** ·THY·SOUL·CHECK·THEE that I come so near,
Swear to thy blind soul that I was thy Will,
And will, thy soul knows, is admitted there;
Thus far for love my love-suit, sweet, fulfil.
Will will fulfil the treasure of thy love—
Ay, fill it full with wills, and my will one.
In things of great receipt with ease we prove
Among a number one is reckoned none:
Then in the number let me pass untold,
Though in thy store's account I one must be;
For nothing hold me, so it please thee hold
That no-thing me a some-thing, sweet, to thee.
    Make but my name thy love, and love that still—
    And then thou lov'st me, for my name is Will.

Sonnet No 136

THOU·BLIND·FOOL·LOVE what dost thou to mine eyes
That they behold, and see not what what they see?
They know what beauty is, see where it lies,
Yet what the best is take the worst to be.
If eyes corrupt by over-partial looks
Be anchored in the bay where all men ride,
Why of eyes' falsehood hast thou forgèd hooks
Whereto the judgement of my heart is tied?
Why should my heart think that a several plot
Which my heart knows the wide world's common place?
Or mine eyes, seeing this, say this is not,
To put fair truth upon so foul a face?
    In things right true my heart and eyes have erred,
    And to this false plague are they now transferred.

Sonnet No 137

WHEN·MY·LOVE·SWEARS that she is made of truth,
I do believe her, though I know she lies,
That she might think me some untutored youth,
Unlearnèd in the world's false subtleties.
Thus vainly thinking that she thinks me young,
Although she knows my days are past the best,
Simply I credit her false-speaking tongue':
On both sides thus is simple truth suppressed.
But wherefore says she not she is unjust?
And wherefore say not I that I am old?
Oh, love's best habit is in seeming trust,
And age in love loves not to have years told.
    Therefore I lie with her, and she with me,
    And in our faults by lies we flattered be.

Sonnet No 138

CALL·ME·NOT to justify the wrong
That thy unkindness lays upon my heart;
  Wound me not with thine eye but with thy tongue;
Use power with power and slay me not by art.
Tell me thou lov'st elsewhere; but in my sight,
Dear heart, forbear to glance thine eye aside;
What need'st thou wound with cunning when thy might
Is more than my o'erpressed defence can bide?
Let me excuse thee: 'Ah, my love well knows
Her pretty looks have been mine enemies,
And therefore from my face she turns my foes,
That they elsewhere might dart their injuries.'
    Yet do not so; but since I am near slain,
    Kill me outright with looks and rid my pain.

Sonnet No 139

B WISE·AS·THOU·ART·CRUEL ; do not press
My tongue-tied patience with too much disdain,
    Lest sorrow lend me words, and words express
The manner of my pity-wanting pain.
If I might teach thee wit, better it were,
Though not to love, yet, love, to tell me so;
As testy sick men, when their deaths be near,
No news but health from their physicians know.
For if I should despair, I should grow mad,
And in my madness might speak ill of thee.
Now this ill-wresting world is grown so bad,
Mad sland'rers by mad ears believèd be.
    That I may not be so, nor thou belied,
    Bear thine eyes straight, though thy proud heart go wide.

Sonnet No 140

IN FAITH, I DO NOT LOVE THEE with mine eyes,
For they in thee a thousand errors note;
But 'tis my heart that loves what they despise,
Who in despite of view is pleased to dote;
Nor are mine ears with thy tongue's tune delighted,
Nor tender feeling to base touches prone;
Nor taste, nor smell, desire to be invited
To any sensual feast with thee alone:
But my five wits nor my five senses can
Dissuade one foolish heart from serving thee,
Who leaves unswayed the likeness of a man,
Thy proud heart's slave and vassal wretch to be:
   Only my plague thus far I count my gain,
   That she that makes me sin awards me pain.

*Sonnet No 141*

LOVE·IS·MY·SIN, and thy dear virtue hate,
Hate of my sin, grounded on sinful loving:
O, but with mine compare thou thine own state
And thou shalt find it merits not reproving;
Or if it do, not from those lips of thine
That have profaned their scarlet ornaments,
And sealed false bonds of love as oft as mine—
Robbed others' beds' revenues of their rents.
Be it lawful I love thee as thou lov'st those
Whom thine eyes woo as mine importune thee:
Root pity in thy heart, that, when it grows,
Thy pity may deserve to pitied be.
    If thou dost seek to have what thou dost hide,
    By self-example mayst thou be denied.

Sonnet No 142

LO AS·A·CAREFUL·HOUSEWIFE runs to catch
One of her feathered creatures broke away,
Sets down her babe and makes all swift dispatch
In pursuit of the thing she would have stay:
Whilst her neglected child holds her in chase,
Cries to catch her whose busy care is bent
To follow that which flies before her face,
Not prizing her poor infant's discontent:
So runn'st thou after that which flies from thee,
Whilst I, thy babe, chase thee afar behind;
But if thou catch thy hope, turn back to me
And play the mother's part — kiss me, be kind.
So will I pray that thou mayst have thy Will,
If thou turn back and my loud crying still.

Sonnet No 143

**TWO · LOVES · I · HAVE**, of comfort and despair,
Which like two spirits do suggest me still:
The better angel is a man right fair,
The worser spirit a woman coloured ill.
To win me soon to hell, my female evil
Tempteth my better angel from my side,
And would corrupt my saint to be a devil,
Wooing his purity with her foul pride.
And whether that my angel be turned fiend
Suspect I may, yet not directly tell;
But being both from me, both to each friend,
I guess one angel in another's hell.
    Yet this shall I ne'er know, but live in doubt
    Till my bad angel fire my good one out.

Sonnet No 144

THOSE·LIPS that Love's own hand did make
Breathed forth the sound that said 'I hate'
To me that languished for her sake:
But when she saw my woeful state,
Straight in her heart did mercy come,
Chiding that tongue that, ever sweet,
Was used in giving gentle doom,
And taught it thus anew to greet:
'I hate' she altered with an end
That followed it as gentle day
Doth follow night, who like a fiend
From heaven to hell is flown away.
    'I hate' from hate away she threw,
    And saved my life, saying: 'not you'.

Sonnet No 145

POOR·SOUL, the centre of my sinful earth,
(Foiled by) these rebel powers that thee array,
Why dost thou pine within and suffer dearth,
Painting thy outward walls so costly gay?
Why so large cost, having so short a lease,
Dost thou upon thy fading mansion spend?
Shall worms, inheritors of this excess,
Eat up thy charge? Is this thy body's end?
Then, soul, live thou upon thy servant's loss,
And let that pine to aggravate thy store;
Buy terms divine in selling hours of dross;
Within be fed, without be rich no more:

So shalt thou feed on Death, that feeds on men,
And Death once dead, there's no more dying then.

Sonnet No 146

MY·LOVE·IS·AS·A·FEVER, longing still
For that which longer nurseth the disease,
Feeding on that which doth preserve the ill,
The uncertain sickly appetite to please.
My reason, the physician to my love,
Angry that his prescriptions are not kept,
Hath left me, and I desperate now approve
Desire is death, which physic did except.
Past cure I am, now reason is past care,
And frantic mad with evermore unrest;
My thoughts and my discourse as madmen's are,
At random from the truth, vainly expressed:
    For I have sworn thee fair, and thought thee bright,
    Who art as black as hell, as dark as night.

Sonnet No 147

O ME! WHAT·EYES·HATH·LOVE put in my head
Which have no correspondence with true sight?
Or if they have, where is my judgement fled,
That censures falsely what they see aright?
If that be fair whereon my false eyes dote,
What means the world to say it is not so?
If it be not, then love doth well denote
Love's eye is not so true as all men's: no,
How can it – oh, how can love's eye be true
That is so vexed with watching and with tears?
No marvel then though I mistake my view
The sun itself sees not till heaven clears.
O cunning love! With tears thou keep'st me blind,
Lest eyes, well seeing, thy foul faults should find.

Sonnet No 148

CANST·THOU,·O·CRUEL, say I love thee not,
    When I against myself with thee partake?
    Do I not think on thee, when I forgot
Am of myself, all tyrant, for thy sake?
Who hateth thee that I do call my friend?
On whom frown'st thou that I do fawn upon?
Nay, if thou lour'st on me, do I not spend
Revenge upon myself with present moan?
What merit do I in myself respect
That is so proud thy service to despise,
When all my best doth worship thy defect,
Commanded by the motion of thine eyes?
    But, love, hate on, for now I know thy mind:
    Those that can see thou lov'st — and I am blind.

Sonnet No 149

FROM what power hast thou this powerful might
With insufficiency my heart to sway,
To make me give the lie to my true sight
And swear that brightness doth not grace the day?
Whence hast thou this becoming of things ill,
That in the very refuse of thy deeds
There is such strength and warrantise of skill
That in my mind thy worst all best exceeds?
Who taught thee how to make me love thee more
The more I hear and see just cause of hate?
Oh, though I love what others do abhor,
With others thou shouldst not abhor my state:
      If thy unworthiness raised love in me
      More worthy I to be beloved of thee.

Sonnet No 150

LOVE is too young to know what conscience is
Yet who knows not conscience is born of love?
Then gentle cheater, urge not my amiss,
Lest guilty of my faults thy sweet self prove:
For, thou betraying me, I do betray
My nobler part to my gross body's treason;
My soul doth tell my body that he may
Triumph in love: flesh stays no farther reason,
But rising at thy name doth point out thee
As his triumphant prize. Proud of this pride,
He is contented thy poor drudge to be,
To stand in thy affairs, fall by thy side.
  No want of conscience hold it that I call
  Her 'love', for whose dear love I rise and fall.

Sonnet No 151

IN·LOVING·THEE thou know'st I am forsworn;
But thou art twice forsworn to me love swearing,
In act thy bed-vow broke, and new faith torn
In vowing new hate after new love bearing.
By why of two oaths' breach do I accuse thee,
When I break twenty? I am perjured most,
For all my vows are oaths but to misuse thee,
And all my honest faith in thee is lost.
For I have sworn deep oaths of thy deep kindness ~
Oaths of thy love, thy truth, thy constancy;
And to enlighten thee gave eyes to blindness,
Or made them swear against the thing they see.
　　For I have sworn thee fair: more perjured eye,
　　To swear against the truth so foul a lie!

Sonnet No 152

CUPID·LAID·BY·HIS·BRAND and fell asleep:
A maid of Dian's this advantage found,
And his love-kindling fire did quickly steep
In a cold valley-fountain of that ground,
Which borrowed from this holy fire of Love
A dateless lively heat, still to endure,
And grew a seething bath which men yet prove
Against strange maladies, a sovereign cure.
But at my mistress' eye Love's brand new fired,
The boy for trial needs would touch my breast:
I, sick withal, the help of bath desired,
And thither hied, a sad distempered guest,
But found no cure: the bath for my help lies
Where Cupid got new fire – my mistress' eyes.

Sonnet No 153

THE·LITTLE·LOVE~GOD lying once asleep,
   Laid by his side his heart-inflaming brand,
   Whilst many nymphs that vowed chaste life to keep
Came tripping by; but in her maiden hand
The fairest votary took up that fire
Which many legions of true hearts had warmed,
And so the General of hot desire
Was, sleeping, by a virgin hand disarmed.
This brand she quenchèd in a cool well by,
Which from Love's fire took heat perpetual,
Growing a bath and healthful remedy
For men diseased. But I, my mistress' thrall,
   Came there for cure, and this by that I prove:
   Love's fire heats water, water cools not love.

Sonnet No 154